ALEXIUS

On this day

A modern meditation on
THE STATIONS OF THE CROSS

THE COLUMBA PRESS
DUBLIN 1992

Introduction

For me, the Stations of the Cross are a meditation on life. We are invited to walk again with Jesus the Way of the Cross. To-day, he continues his painful journey among our brothers and sisters who are being condemned, kidnapped, starved, abandoned, aborted, tortured and killed day after day all over the world.

The Way of the Cross is Franciscan in origin. When the early followers of St Francis asked him to teach them about prayer, he spoke about the book of the cross. All the lessons they would ever need could be read on the cross of Jesus Christ.

It is certainly true that the passion of Christ can teach us one important lesson, namely how to cope with the hardships of life. So much modern jargon evades the pain of living. I believe that what is needed most to combat the mystery of evil is to reflect again on the sufferings of Christ, the lonely desertion he suffered and the values he found in taking up his cross and sticking with it. Under the weight of so much pre-sent day stress, the memory of Calvary may very well be the only motive we have left for remaining steadfast.

The following meditations were first delivered as Good Friday Stations of the Cross in the Capuchin Church of the Holy Trinity, Cork. Hence the title *On this day*. May this booklet enable many to pray the Way of the Cross with sincerity and devotion.

Alexius Healy, OFM Capuchin

Opening Prayer

Lord,
we are about to walk in prayer
the Way of the Cross with you.
You bore our faults
in your body on the cross.
Through your wounds
may we find healing;
through your suffering
may we find peace;
through your dying
may we be born to
everlasting Life.
Through your passion and death
may we be brought
to the glory of the resurrection.

FIRST STATION
Jesus is condemned to death

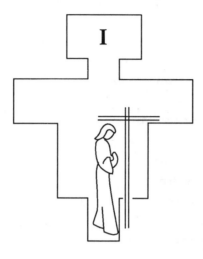

We adore you, Lord Jesus Christ,
and we bless you,
because by your holy cross
you have redeemed the world.

This is a scene found to-day in many of our countries torn apart by war and bloodshed. In the city of Jerusalem there are riots, marches, protests. Terrorists pave the street. Shouts of 'Crucify him, crucify him,' ring loud and clear. Suddenly there is a hushed silence. Christ appears at the door of Pilate's courtroom – a man alone and condemned. Pressure groups have won the day. Jesus must die, a human life must be destroyed.

Lord,
grant us the grace not to condemn life
but to accept and respect it.
Human life is sacred from womb to tomb;
no motive
can ever make its destruction right.
Enlighten those
who exploit the dignity of human life
to see the futility of violence and murder.
May the gift of your Spirit
lead us to recognise,
across all frontiers,
the faces of our brothers and sisters,
children of God,
our Father in heaven.

Dying you destroyed our death.
Rising you restored our life.
Lord Jesus, come in glory.

SECOND STATION
Jesus accepts his cross

We adore you, Lord Jesus Christ,
and we bless you,
because by your holy cross
you have redeemed the world.

'If any man has a mind to come after me, let him take up his cross daily and follow me.' Jesus goes forward with great courage to do his Father's will: 'Thy will be done not mine.' He accepts the cross to teach us how precious we are in the eyes of God. His grace can transform every cross we meet into a victory of love.

Lord,
your Gospel does not promise
that we will be spared from pain.
Help us to understand
that no matter how we try
to escape the cross
it remains a human reality,
but your life
gives meaning to it.
You saw
that it was necessary
to pass through pain and death
and bowed your head
to the Father's will.
Keep us from bitterness
and despair.
Teach us to come prayerfully,
in poverty of spirit,
with open hands.
Give us the grace of acceptance
and resignation.
Help us to accept reality,
to live with ourselves
and our crosses.

Dying you destroyed our death.
Rising you restored our life.
Lord Jesus, come in glory.

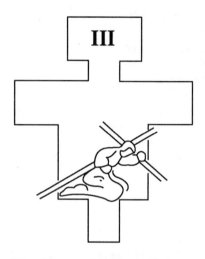

We adore you, Lord Jesus Christ,
and we bless you,
because by your holy cross
you have redeemed the world.

Christ is now on his way to the hill of Calvary. The road is long, the paved street is rough and the heat of the noonday sun is overpowering. He arrives at the foot of the hill. He has left the level ground and starts to climb. It now becomes more difficult. He grows weary beneath the heavy weight, stumbles and falls.

Lord,
your first fall
is like the fall of the young person
on the threshold of adolescence.
There are many new challenges
and temptations now.
Give courage and strength to the young.
Help them to avoid wrong-doing.
Protect them
from drunkenness, drugs and permissiveness.
Teach them to handle their problems
with gentleness,
without panic or self-pity.
Help us, who lead them,
to build an environment of love and trust
where they will make
the right decisions for their future.
When their youthful idealism is shattered
by sin and human weakness,
give them the grace
to rise from their fall and try again.

Dying you destroyed our death.
Rising you restored our life.
Lord Jesus, come in glory.

We adore you, Lord Jesus Christ,
and we bless you,
because by your holy cross
you have redeemed the world.

A Mother meets a son. Mary encounters Jesus. It is a soul-piercing experience. She is there at the right time, in the right place. She offers encouragement and sympathy, aware that her son is fulfilling his Father's will.

Mary,
you were human,
a woman who knew the pain and hard knocks of life.
Your son gave you to us
to be our mother.
Gentle Mary, we mothers
are often torn between anguish and hope,
baffled at seeing our children suffer,
tempted to think that we have failed our families
and that God has abandoned us.
Give to women
a calm vision of life.
Teach them their true role in modern society.
May they be Christ-bearers,
evangelisers in the home,
in the community, in the workplace,
maintaining and restoring life and love.
Mary, our mother,
protect the gift of innocence
in today's youth.
Mirror of Justice, Queen of Peace,
be with us now
and at the hour of our death.

Dying you destroyed our death.
Rising you restored our life.
Lord Jesus, come in glory.

FIFTH STATION
Simon helps Jesus carry his cross

We adore you, Lord Jesus Christ,
and we bless you,
because by your holy cross
you have redeemed the world.

The cross is becoming too heavy for Jesus. A passer-by is forced to help lighten the burden. Christ accepts gratefully. Christ needed Simon. That small gesture of charity would never be forgotten.

Lord,
we sometimes find it burdensome
to involve ourselves with people.
Teach us that the essence of Christianity is love;
that every person is our neighbour.
Let us see your presence
in all people.
Help us to recognise you especially
in the poor, the sick and the elderly.
May we do the menial tasks
that no one else will take on.
Make us humble enough to accept help
from others.
Thank you, Lord,
for the good neighbours and friends
who bring us
sunshine and laughter and love.

Dying you destroyed our death.
Rising you restored our life.
Lord Jesus, come in glory.

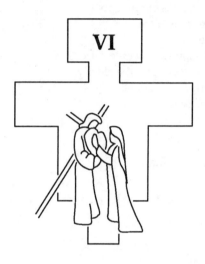

We adore you, Lord Jesus Christ,
and we bless you,
because by your holy cross
you have redeemed the world.

A woman steps out from the crowd. Gently but courageously, Veronica wipes the face of Jesus. She braves threats, verbal abuse and even violence. In gratitude, Jesus signs her towel with the imprint of his face.

Lord,
fear often makes us run away
from demanding situations.
Give us the strength
not to be swayed
by the company we are in,
by the fashions of the times,
by the desire to foolishly follow the crowd.
Help us
to speak out
when Christian values are at stake.
Give us the courage
to follow our own consciences
no matter what others may think or say.
Keep us faithful
to your teaching.
Grant us the grace
to accept the difficulties
of sometimes having to stand alone
in defending justice and truth.

Dying you destroyed our death.
Rising you restored our life.
Lord Jesus, come in glory.

SEVENTH STATION
Jesus falls the second time

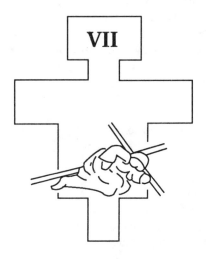

We adore you, Lord Jesus Christ,
and we bless you,
because by your holy cross
you have redeemed the world.

*The second fall of Jesus might well be compared to the trials and
stresses of middle-age. Christ is not as strong now as when he first
began to climb the hill of Calvary. He stumbles and falls. But in rising
again and struggling on, he challenges us to begin anew each time
we fall.*

Lord,
when we are drained and discouraged
from continual frustration and setbacks,
give us strength to accept ourselves
with humble patience.
A person is not a failure because he falls.
When life seems to crumble
and we imagine that we are useless and unimportant,
help us to our feet again.
Listen to the cry of our brokenness and confusion;
help us to rise with dignity
and begin again.
May we never despair of your love and forgiveness,
let us pass this supreme hope on to others.

Dying you destroyed our death.
Rising you restored our life.
Lord Jesus, come in glory.

Jesus speaks to the women and children

We adore you, Lord Jesus Christ,
and we bless you,
because by your holy cross
you have redeemed the world.

*Along the Way of the Cross, there were women who wept in pity.
Jesus accepted their compassion but mysteriously warned, 'Weep
first for yourselves and your children.' He foresaw the sad things to
come. People would choose to remain in sin and reject the healing
power of God's forgiveness.*

God of mercy and compassion,
teach us
that even if our hearts condemn us
you do not come to reject us,
but to reveal yourself
as the God of immense tenderness.
In your providence,
all things co-operate for good;
even, in a mysterious way,
our sins.
Lord of infinite mercy,
our future lies in your hands.
All we really need
is a contrite, humble heart
coming back to you.
Stretch out your hand in blessing,
in pardon and in peace.

Dying you destroyed our death.
Rising you restored our life.
Lord Jesus, come in glory.

NINTH STATION
Jesus falls the third time

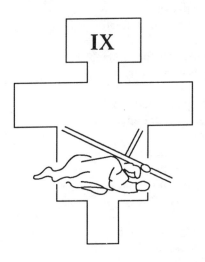

We adore you, Lord Jesus Christ,
and we bless you,
because by your holy cross
you have redeemed the world.

*It is difficult to be old in an uncaring world where many feel that
the aged have nothing to offer. This station gives hope to the old, to
the depressed and to those who have given up on life. Christ is near
the end of the road and is completely drained of strength. This time
it is more difficult to rise. 'My God, my God, why hast thou forsak-
en me?' But he gets up and staggers on.*

Lord of all hopefulness,
bring to the sick
your comfort and healing.
Be to the old
and bedridden
their stay and companion.
Teach patient tolerance
to all who are no longer young.
Give to the dying
the grace of perseverance
which you won for them
in your third fall,
the assurance
that when the final moments of life
ebb away
you will come
and take them to yourself.

Dying you destroyed our death.
Rising you restored our life.
Lord Jesus, come in glory.

We adore you, Lord Jesus Christ,
and we bless you,
because by your holy cross
you have redeemed the world.

Jesus is stripped not just of his cloak but of his dignity, his respect, his rights. Stripped and naked, our Saviour waits patiently for what is to come. He is a poor man and the poor must always wait. His nakedness challenges our affluent society with its false standards and shallow values.

Lord,
you know the loneliness
of the empty chair,
the parting with loved ones,
the going away of children.
Lord, help us
when sickness seems to strip away
our protections and
nails us to a bed of pain.
Strengthen us
when all the support
we have in life
– family, health and possessions –
are taken away
and we stand there raw and bleeding
because these things
have been so much a part of us.
Lord, let us remember
this moment of your passion
and be consoled.

Dying you destroyed our death.
Rising you restored our life.
Lord Jesus, come in glory.

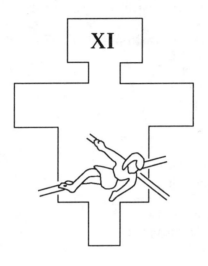

We adore you, Lord Jesus Christ,
and we bless you,
because by your holy cross
you have redeemed the world.

Our eyes almost refuse to look on this most appalling aspect of Christ's passion. Hammers are raised, blows descend, iron spikes tear their way through his flesh. His muscles spasm and stiffen. The crowd taunt him with madness and failure and folly. Jesus prays for his murderers: 'Father forgive them ...'

Lord, our God,
we ask you to forgive us
for the suffering that we cause to others,
for our lack of understanding,
for nursing grudges,
for keeping up resentments,
for not admitting when we are wrong,
for the bitterness and spite
we often feel towards others.
Create a new heart in us,
give us a spirit of reconciliation and forgiveness.
Where sin has brought division and enmity,
may your love bring healing and strength;
where sin has brought death,
may the grace of your passion and death
bring new life.

Dying you destroyed our death.
Rising you restored our life.
Lord Jesus, come in glory.

We adore you, Lord Jesus Christ,
and we bless you,
because by your holy cross
you have redeemed the world.

Jesus, crying out in a loud voice, said, 'Father, into your hands I commend my spirit.' And having said this, he breathed his last. This is the Gospel passage which recalls the hour of supreme sacrifice. Love in all its beauty has reached a climax; the lover has given his life for his beloved.

Lord,
you are the Suffering Servant.
You preached peace and reconciliation,
yet, you were treated like a fool,
with utter disrespect
with blows and beatings,
stripped of everything,
abandoned by all,
dying the death of a slave.
O Jesus, Wounded Healer,
we place our trust in you;
your entry into glory is our hope of heaven.
Let us know your peace
at the hour of death.
May we be prepared and willing to go
when you call us from this world
to our eternal home in heaven.

Dying you destroyed our death.
Rising you restored our life.
Lord Jesus, come in glory.

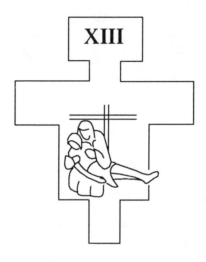

We adore you, Lord Jesus Christ,
and we bless you,
because by your holy cross
you have redeemed the world.

*Joseph and Nicodemus took down the body of Jesus from the cross
and placed it in his mother's arms. Mary gazed on the wounds in
his hands and feet and side. Christ still bears these wounds in his
risen and glorified body. They are a pledge of his powerful interces-
sion on our behalf before the throne of God.*

Lord,
we look on your wounded hands.
We think of our own hands,
lazy, idle, sinful hands.
Your wounded feet recall
your journeys of mercy.
We think of our feet
that have often gone astray.
Your wounded side reveals a heart
that was broken for love of us.
May your wounds help us to live
with a sense of responsibility.
Teach us to appreciate
the Eucharist and Confession,
to love you with intensity and sincerity.
Grant us patience
to accept our own wounds with resignation.

Dying you destroyed our death.
Rising you restored our life.
Lord Jesus, come in glory.

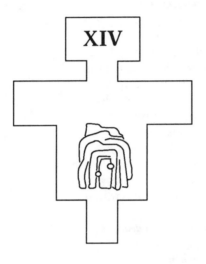

We adore you, Lord Jesus Christ,
and we bless you,
because by your holy cross
you have redeemed the world.

The hill of Calvary is the symbol of liberation and hope. Each new ridge we conquer opens up new insights into the beauty of God. The summit is the prize: heaven, where the sun and scorching wind cannot touch us any more, where the lamb will lead us to springs of living water, where God will wipe away all tears from our eyes.

Lord,
as we lay our loved ones to rest
let us remember that pain and suffering
have no power over them.
Give resignation and peace to all who mourn.
By your cross and resurrection
you have set us free.
Thank you,
for being a Saviour
for each and every one of us.
Yes, Lord, we firmly believe that
you have gone to prepare a place for us
so that where you are,
we also may be.
We shall always be with the Lord.
Let us console one another
with these words.

Dying you destroyed our death.
Rising you restored our life.
Lord Jesus, come in glory.

Closing Prayer

Lord, God,
when our world lay in ruins
you raised it up again
through your passion and death.
Lord of the sun and the stars,
we celebrate with joy
the glory of your resurrection,
for through it
the world is flooded with light.
O King of the Friday,
whose limbs
were stretched on the cross,
O Lord, who suffered
the bruises, the wounds, the loss,
we lay ourselves open
to the loving kindness
of your Sacred Heart.
May some fruit
from the tree of your passion
fall upon us *On this day.*